DATE DUE

MAR 1 0 2014		
OCT 2 1 2015		
NOV 1 9 2015		
OCT 2 5 2017		

The Library Store #47-0152

STORIES
WELL TOLD

PUBLISHED *by* Creative Education
P.O. Box 227, Mankato, Minnesota 56002
Creative Education is an imprint of The Creative Company
www.thecreativecompany.us

DESIGN AND PRODUCTION *by* Ellen Huber
ART DIRECTION *by* Rita Marshall
PRINTED *in the* United States of America

PHOTOGRAPHS *by*
Alamy (AF archive, Geo Images, Moviestore collection Ltd,
Photos 12), Corbis (Bettmann, Sunset Boulevard),
Getty Images (Chad Baker, Jonathan Barry, Ivan Bliznetsov,
Jan Hakan Dahlstrom, Purestock, Marti Saiz, SuperStock, United Artists),
Shutterstock (Brad Collett, Michael Jaszewski,
Johnna Evang Nonboe), SuperStock (SuperStock)

ILLUSTRATIONS
page 10 © 1990 Roberto Innocenti; pages 21, 31 © 1996 Gary Kelley

Library of Congress Cataloging-in-Publication Data
Bodden, Valerie.
Horror / Valerie Bodden.
p. cm. — (Stories well told)
Includes bibliographical references and index.
Summary: A survey of the horror fiction genre, from its folkloric origins and Gothic influences
to the famous authors—such as Stephen King—whose works have defined the genre over time.

ISBN 978-1-60818-180-3
1. Horror tales—History and criticism—Juvenile literature. I. Title.

PN3435.B63 2012
809.3'8738—dc23   2012023239

First Edition
2 4 6 8 9 7 5 3 1

VALERIE BODDEN

HORROR

CREATIVE EDUCATION

TABLE OF CONTENTS

WIND WHEEZES THROUGH CRACKS IN THE WINDOWPANES, MAKING THE HOUSE SOUND AS THOUGH IT IS BREATHING.

—◆—

A steady rain thrums against the glass, occasionally picking up speed with the gusting wind, then slowing again to the sharp rhythm of tapping fingernails. The house is dark except for a lone candle in an upstairs room. The candle dimly illuminates damp walls, their neglected wallpaper peeling to reveal red paint that might once have been bright but now looks like dried blood. A thick layer of dust rests on the room's few furnishings. Only the desk upon which the candle sits is clean. Here, papers have been spread out, and a pale hand quickly scratches a pen back and forth across a sheet. The writer stares intently at the words of the story he is writing. To Edgar Allan Poe, an atmosphere of dread is all part of a day's—or night's—work.

Horror stories can best be defined by the feeling they produce in readers: fear. In order to inspire this fear, horror stories feature monsters. These monsters can range from vampires, werewolves, and witches to madmen, guilt-ridden consciences, and unseen, unidentified presences.

Stories containing elements of horror form part of the folklore of nearly every human culture ever recorded. Some of the oldest surviving examples of horror in Western literature come from the *Odyssey*, written by the Greek poet Homer around 800 B.C. The long poem (divided into 24 books) relates the heroic deeds of the brave king Odysseus. In Book IX, Odysseus describes the horrifying acts of Polyphemus, a giant, one-eyed monster known as a Cyclops: "With a sudden clutch he gripped up two of my men at once and dashed them down upon the ground.... The earth was wet with their blood. Then he tore them limb from limb and supped upon [ate] them."

Similar stories of horrifying monsters and dreadful deeds appear in many tales, up through the works of early 17th-century English playwright William Shakespeare. Although such episodes helped to lay the foundation of the horror story, the genre in its current form began to develop in the mid-1700s. European authors writing in the newly popular literary form of the novel began to pen entire works aimed at arousing fear, dread, or awe in readers. Such novels, known as Gothic romances, often featured forbidding castles, supernatural occurrences, and distressed heroines.

The first Gothic novel is generally considered to be *The Castle of Otranto* (1764), by British author Horace Walpole. As the novel opens, the prince Manfred discovers that his 15-year-old son, who was about to be married to the princess Isabella, has been killed by an enormous helmet that has fallen from the sky—and

< 8 >

Four ghosts pay visits to Scrooge in A Christmas Carol, *the first of which is the transparent spirit of his former business partner, Jacob Marley.*

no explanation is given for why or how the helmet came to be there. Afterward, Manfred decides that he will marry Isabella himself. However, the unwilling young woman flees in terror through the castle's underground passages: "An awful silence reigned throughout those subterraneous [underground] regions, except now and then some blasts of wind that shook the doors she had passed, and which, grating on the rusty hinges, were re-echoed through that long labyrinth [maze] of darkness. Every murmur struck her with new terror." Scenes of suspense and terror set in old castles or haunted houses soon became a hallmark of the Gothic genre.

Although such sensational occurrences earned Gothic novels a low reputation among literary critics, the works were immensely popular with readers. Hundreds of Gothic novels were published in England, America, Germany, and France in the wake of *The Castle of Otranto*. In some, readers were introduced to new types of monsters. British author Mary Wollstonecraft Shelley's *Frankenstein; or, The Modern Prometheus* (1818), for example, introduced a creature assembled from parts of corpses. Although the popularity of Gothic novels had begun to fade by about 1820, many writers continued to produce Gothic short stories, which were published in magazines such as Scotland's *Blackwood's Edinburgh Magazine*.

As the Gothic novel lost its hold, many horror writers shifted their focus to psychological, rather than purely physical, horrors. In many ghost stories, for example, fear was aroused not by the ghosts themselves but by the guilty consciences of the characters to whom they appeared. In British author Charles Dickens's *A Christmas Carol* (1843), Ebenezer Scrooge is warned by the ghost of his former business partner that he faces an eternity filled with the "torture of remorse," if he does not begin to show compassion for others.

Other authors played on fears common to the age, including those of being buried alive or of going insane. Such themes were especially prominent in the

A HORROR CHARACTER

The monster or villain in a horror story has to be sinister, scary, and intimidating—in short, horrible. Although horror monsters can come in nearly any form imaginable, modern master Stephen King professes that there are four basic monster archetypes. The first is the vampire, which includes any monster that preys upon people. Another archetype is the monster that appears to be a normal person but transforms into an evil being. A werewolf, for example, turns into a dangerous monster at the full moon, and a serial killer may sometimes act like a normal person. Ghosts are the third archetype. These supernatural beings often reflect the evil of the person they torment. Finally, some horror monsters fit into the category King calls the "Thing Without a Name," which includes man-made monsters as well as unknown threats.

No matter what their type, horror monsters generally manifest evil in one form or another, and they tend to be powerful. In many cases, horror stories revolve around the attempt to defeat a nearly unbeatable monster, lending a sense of urgency to the work. Among the most famous of horror monsters is the creature fashioned by Dr. Frankenstein in Mary Wollstonecraft Shelley's **Frankenstein**. Despite the atrocities he commits, Frankenstein's monster at times comes across as a sympathetic character because he has been shunned by the very person who created him. The demonic character of Randall Flagg in Stephen King's **The Stand** (1978), by contrast, is pure evil, bringing destruction wherever and whenever he can throughout the ages—and enjoying it.

< 12 >

Vampires are sometimes depicted as giant bat-like monsters, as the vampire Dracula is in a pivotal scene from the 2004 movie Van Helsing.

works of American author Edgar Allan Poe, who wrote in a Gothic mode yet emphasized not only haunted buildings and supernatural occurrences but also haunted minds, mental drama, and psychological symbolism. Among the most famous of the tormented minds in his works is the narrator of "The Tell-Tale Heart" (1843), who insists that he is sane: "True!—nervous—very, very dreadfully nervous I had been and am; but why *will* you say that I am mad? ... I heard all things in the heaven and in the earth. I heard many things in hell. How, then, am I mad?" By the end of the tale, readers learn the true extent of the narrator's insanity: he has killed a man and buried him under the floorboards of his house.

The final decades of the 19th century saw a revival of interest in Gothic themes, most notably with the 1897 publication of Irish writer Bram Stoker's classic vampire novel *Dracula*. Already popular in its day, the work has since gained a reputation as the most influential horror novel of all time. With the exception of *Dracula* and a few other novels, however, the short story form dominated works in the horror genre during the late 19th and early 20th centuries.

By the early 1900s, the ghost story was in its prime in England in the works of author M. R. James, whose antiquarian tales (which often involved the discovery of an old book or other ancient object) raised the possibility of accidentally unleashing ancient supernatural beings onto modern society. Around the same time, other authors began to write stories that were later labeled as cosmic horror. Such horror presented a chaotic, hostile universe filled with secret terrors that humans were helpless to overcome. The cosmic story reached its peak in the works of American author H. P. Lovecraft, whose fictional universe known as the Cthulhu Mythos fused inner, psychological terror with an outer, cosmic threat posed by monstrous alien creatures.

< 14 >

Legends of and superstitions about vampires spread from eastern to western Europe in the 1700s, generating stories that inspired Stoker's Dracula.

Like many horror stories of the time, Lovecraft's works were first published in *Weird Tales*, one of the many American "pulp" magazines popular from the 1920s until the 1940s. Named for the cheap, wood-pulp paper on which they were printed, the pulps published new fiction as well as reprints of older horror stories. Sold for 10 to 25 cents an issue, the pulps reached a wide readership.

By the 1950s, pulp magazines had largely faded from the scene, and in the 1960s and '70s, a number of horror authors turned back to the novel form. Many reworked the Gothic tradition to create new genres of horror, with tales populated by ecological terrors, sociopaths, and new versions of old monsters. For the first time, horror writers began to find their works regularly atop bestseller lists.

In the 1980s and '90s, horror novelists working in the new splatterpunk movement filled their books with shocking scenes of violence, gore, and death. By the late '90s, however, a new generation of horror writers had begun to experiment with the genre, ignoring or reworking its traditions to fit their own needs and playing with stylistic elements such as point of view. Although many of today's horror novels continue to feature supernatural creatures, they increasingly take place in the everyday world, bringing horror directly into readers' lives.

The majority of those readers are teenagers and young adults. This audience can easily identify with modern horror's protagonists, who are often adolescents like themselves. Whatever their age, horror readers have one thing in common, though: they want to be surprised, shocked, and scared—in short, horrified.

< 16 >

Although the goal of nearly every horror story is to produce fear, not all horror stories accomplish this in the same way. The horror genre can be divided into a number of subgenres (or subcategories), each with its own features and focus. Perhaps the easiest way to subdivide the genre is by the types of monsters that predominate in a story.

Since the first Gothic novels of the 1700s, many horror stories have featured ghosts and haunted houses. Ghosts may seek retribution for a past wrong, or they may serve to protect the living. Haunted houses are generally haunted because of events that either happened within them or on the land upon which they were built. American author Shirley Jackson's novel *The Haunting of Hill House* (1959) is a classic haunted-house story. In it, unseen spirits haunt the Hill House mansion, and the house itself eventually seems to possess one of its visitors, Eleanor, whom the other characters finally convince to leave. As she prepares to do so, she looks back up "at the amused, certain face of the house, watching her quietly. The house was waiting now, she thought, and it was waiting for her; no one else could satisfy it." As Eleanor drives away, she crashes into a tree on the property and is killed. The reader is left with an eerie sensation that the final descriptions of Hill House as "not sane" and "holding darkness within" are true.

Like ghosts and haunted houses, vampires are featured in many horror stories. Originally, the vampire was depicted as a hideous, monstrous creature, but today's vampires are often presented as sympathetic—and even romantic—characters who are not all that different from the victims whose blood they drink. In American writer Anne Rice's 1976 novel *Interview with the Vampire*, for example, the vampire Louis is at first horrified at the idea of feeding on humans. Although he later begins to drink human blood, he retains a level of humanity as he cares for his vampire "daughter" Claudia.

A mummy is simply a preserved body, and many cultures around the
world—from Egypt to China to South America—historically mummified their dead.

Vampires are often described as "undead" (technically dead but still animate), as are other monsters such as mummies and zombies. The mummy subgenre gained popularity after the discovery of King Tut's tomb in Egypt in 1922. Two years later, the death of the archaeologist who had discovered the tomb was blamed by many on a curse—and such curses often appear in mummy stories. Mummies are often awoken by accident. They may search for a specific item that will bring them peace in the afterlife, or they might seek revenge on the person who disturbed them. Like mummies, zombies can be reanimated by accident (through an environmental factor such as radiation, for example), or they can be revived on purpose. In American author Stephen King's *Pet Sematary* (1983), for example, the dead are intentionally buried in an ancient American Indian burial ground that allows them to come back to life—but only as dangerous variations of their former selves. Zombies are often portrayed as slow-moving, unthinking, gory-looking creatures that feed on human flesh and brains. Similar to mummies and zombies (but not "undead") are golems, or artificially created beings with no soul. Like the most famous golem of them all—Frankenstein's nameless monster— most golems eventually revolt and torment or kill their creator.

In contrast to the soulless golem, the monster in other works is a living human being whose soul has been possessed by demonic forces. In many cases, the person possessed is simply an innocent victim, as in American author William Peter Blatty's *The Exorcist* (1971), which portrays the possession of a 12-year-old girl after a priest unearths powerful demonic relics. In other horror stories, demons torment characters without ever possessing them, sometimes compelling the characters to "sell" their souls to gain what they want or need.

While supernatural forces such as demons have figured in the horror genre from the beginning, a more recent subgenre depicts ordinary humans as

< 19 >

A HORROR ACTIVITY

Horror authors are experts in creating an atmosphere, or feeling, of dread. But different authors use different techniques to call up that dread. Some rely on descriptions of eerie settings or a slow buildup of tension, while others focus on the twisted thoughts of demented characters. In order to get a feeling for the atmosphere of a horror story, read several paragraphs of works by different horror authors. You might look at "The Fall of the House of Usher" (1839) by Edgar Allan Poe for an example of a dark setting or at Robert Bloch's Psycho *(1959) for insight into the mind of a sociopath. William Hope Hodgson's "The Voice in the Night" (1907) creates a slow-mounting fear as it describes the transformation of humans into a bizarre fungus. As you read each author's work, pay attention to whether one makes you feel more scared or "creeped out" than another. Why do you think that is?*

Now, can you rewrite one of the less scary passages to make it more frightening? For example, if you find Hodgson's lengthy buildup of suspense in the introduction to his story less than terrifying, think about ways that it could become scarier. Would it be more frightening if there was less dialogue and more action? Try writing it that way. Or do you think the character of Norman Bates from Psycho *would be even scarier in a creepier setting? Where? Write him a new backdrop. After you've finished, show your improvements to a teacher, friend, or relative. If they're scared, you've succeeded!*

< 20 >

Poe uses the moody words "dull," "dark," "dreary," "soundless," and "oppressively" in the first sentence to set the stage for the "melancholy House of Usher."

Perhaps the most popular monster in all of horror fiction is Frankenstein's monster,
who was brought to movie life by actor Boris Karloff in 1931.

the monsters. In the maniac subgenre of horror, the monster is a disturbed, often sociopathic person who turns against family, friends, or strangers—in many cases after experiencing a traumatic childhood. *Hannibal Rising* (2006) by American author Thomas Harris, for example, implies that the character Hannibal Lecter becomes a serial killer and cannibal (as chronicled in Harris's 1981 novel *Red Dragon* and 1988's *The Silence of the Lambs*) because of the violent events he witnessed as a child—including the death of his sister at the hands of German Nazi supporters, who fed on her body.

For the past 40 years, the subgenre of technohorror has been growing along with the pace of the rapid advances in technology. In this type of horror, the threat comes not from a monster or a person but rather from science or technology. For example, machines might turn against people, as in American writer Dean Koontz's *Demon Seed* (1973), in which a computer imprisons a young woman in her home. Or science experiments may go terribly wrong, producing horrible results, as is the case in *Frankenstein*.

In place of an outside threat, the psychological subgenre of horror deals with inner, psychological torment, which can result from mental illness, abuse, or guilt over former actions. Despite its lack of monsters, this subgenre can produce an equal—or even greater—feeling of terror. Some works leave readers with the unsettling question of whether the story "really" happened. For example, in American writer Tananarive Due's *The Between* (1995), the protagonist is forced to wonder if he is truly alive—or if he died in a childhood accident he had thought he survived.

Although it may seem surprising, horror fiction also often contains elements of humor. Comic horror seeks to make readers laugh at their fears, often by parodying more traditional works of horror, as in British author Jane Austen's

< 23 >

Northanger Abbey (1817). After reading too many Gothic novels, the protagonist, Catherine, imagines herself the helpless heroine of one of the stories. One night, while a guest in a former abbey, she discovers a hidden roll of papers that she is sure must contain some horrifying secret, but before she can read them, she accidentally extinguishes her candle and becomes "motionless with horror.... Catherine trembled from head to foot.... A cold sweat stood on her forehead, the manuscript fell from her hand, and groping her way to the bed, she jumped hastily in, and sought some suspensions of agony by creeping far underneath the clothes [blankets]." In the morning, Catherine finds that the papers she had dropped in dread were only laundry bills and other unimportant receipts.

More than many other fiction genres, horror lends itself well to the short story form. In fact, some of the greatest masterpieces of horror fiction are short stories, since the brief format allows for the creation of a concentrated, convincing atmosphere of terror. Such a mood can be felt in British author William Hope Hodgson's "The Voice in the Night," in which a man and his fiancée are marooned on a deserted island and soon find an eerie, gray fungus growing on their bodies. When the protagonist discovers "an extraordinarily shaped mass of fungus" that moves and has "a grotesque resemblance to the figure of a distorted human creature," he concludes that this is what will eventually become of himself and his beloved as well.

Oftentimes, and especially at night, people can convince themselves that they

In 1764, a book that would later earn fame as the first Gothic novel was published anonymously in London and became an immediate success. When a second edition of *The Castle of Otranto* was released, the author signed his name to it. The Gothic inventor was Horace Walpole, son of the first British prime minister, Sir Robert Walpole. Horace, who was fascinated with all things medieval, had renovated his house, Strawberry Hill, in the Gothic style, eventually adding small towers, cloisters, and protective walls called battlements to the structure. Walpole's fascination with Gothic architecture is reflected in his novel's haunted castle—complete with trap doors, slimy passages, and bleeding statues—through which the half-evil protagonist Manfred chases the helpless Isabella. Walpole's fictional castle, along with its natural and supernatural devices, provided the model for the buildings featured in nearly all Gothic novels to come.

British author Ann Radcliffe was among the first to employ and expand upon Walpole's haunted castles. Radcliffe began to write in her early 20s to occupy her time while her husband worked late. Although a private person by nature, she became the most popular author in England with her 1794 novel *The Mysteries of Udolpho*. The tale is set largely in the castle Udolpho, which seems to take on a life of its own as the protagonist, Emily St. Aubert, views it for the first time: "Silent, lonely and sublime, it seemed to stand the sovereign [ruler] of the scene, and to frown defiance on all, who dared to invade its solitary reign." Instead of using truly supernatural elements, Radcliffe plays on the heroine's fears to create suspense. For instance, when Emily finds a black veil covering a wall in the castle, she pulls it aside and faints. Suspense builds as Emily's—and the reader's—suspicions run wild regarding the horrors the castle might hold. After 400 pages, readers finally learn what Emily saw—a wax figure (which she had taken to be real) of a dead body, with its face half eaten by worms.

< 26 >

In contrast to Radcliffe's suspenseful works, the novels of British author Matthew Gregory Lewis induce physical horror through the presentation of gruesome and violent acts. Lewis wrote his best-known work, *The Monk* (1796), at the age of 19. In this novel, there is no mystery and no explaining away the supernatural, for Lewis's monsters are real, and they are horrifying. *The Monk* details the downfall of Ambrosio, a monk who is tempted into sin by a disguised servant of Satan. In order to escape punishment, Ambrosio sells his soul to the devil, leading to a gory ending in which he is dropped onto rocks from a great height and left to die in the sun, with insects and eagles feeding on his body. Although *The Monk* was a popular success, it was criticized by reviewers as immoral. In 1798, Lewis (by then a member of the British Parliament) released a revised version with more moderate language, changing words such as "lust" to "desire," for example.

Although trained as a lawyer, American Charles Brockden Brown left the law to pursue a literary career in which he adapted the Gothic form for an American audience and setting. In place of the haunted castles of European Gothic works, Brown uses haunted forests or the plague-ridden city of Philadelphia, Pennsylvania. The apparently supernatural in Brown's works is explained away by science. A mysterious voice heard by characters in *Wieland; or, The Transformation* (1798), for example, comes from a ventriloquist. In addition, many of Brown's works focus on the psychological aspects of horror, casting doubts on the reliability of their storytellers. Brown's psychological focus and American Gothic settings would later be taken up by writers such as Edgar Allan Poe and Nathaniel Hawthorne.

In 1816, 19-year-old Mary Wollstonecraft Shelley began to write what would become her first novel for a ghost-story contest involving herself, her soon-to-be husband (British poet Percy Bysshe Shelley), and their friend,

< 29 >

A HORROR MASTER

Born in Boston, Massachusetts, in 1809, Edgar Allan Poe was raised by a wealthy merchant family in Virginia following his mother's 1811 death. After studying at the University of Virginia for a year, Poe published his first book, Tamerlane and Other Poems *(1827), at the age of 18. He then served briefly in the U.S. Army before becoming a short story writer. Beginning in 1835, he served as the editor of a number of magazines, in which he published both short stories and literary reviews. In 1845, Poe gained national fame with the publication of his poem "The Raven." Two years later, Poe was devastated by the death of his wife, Virginia. He died in 1849 of causes that remain unknown today.*

Although Poe wrote primarily in the Gothic tradition, his horror stories focused on terrors of the mind, such as the guilty conscience, the fear of being buried alive, and the terror of impending death. In "The Pit and the Pendulum" (1842), for example, a prisoner of the Spanish Inquisition awaits a torturous death as a large, sharp pendulum is slowly lowered toward his heart: "Down—still unceasingly—still inevitably down! I gasped and struggled at each vibration. I shrunk convulsively at its every sweep." Poe's dark works influenced countless horror writers in the generations to come, among them H. P. Lovecraft, Robert Bloch, and Stephen King. In addition to writing some of the best-known horror stories ever, Poe is credited with inventing the detective story and with penning some of the earliest works of science fiction.

After Poe realized his
young wife was fatally
afflicted with tuberculosis,
he wrote some of his darkest
and best stories, including
"The Tell-Tale Heart."

British poet Lord Byron. The result was *Frankenstein; or, The Modern Prometheus*, which introduced one of the most famous horror monsters of all time. Shelley's novel presents the scientist Victor Frankenstein, who has created a giant man from parts of dead bodies. Although Frankenstein attempts to make his creature beautiful, he ends up with a yellow-skinned, watery-eyed, black-lipped monster. Repulsed by his "child," he abandons it, but the rejected creature takes revenge on its creator, killing Frankenstein's brother and fiancée. Shelley's novel led to the creation of an entire subgenre of horror featuring Frankenstein's monster.

The works of British sisters Charlotte and Emily Brontë contain horror of a more subtle nature. When the sisters published their first novels in 1847, they adopted the respective pen names of Currer and Ellis Bell in order to avoid the biased treatment often received by women writers at the time. While Charlotte's *Jane Eyre* met with immediate success, Emily's *Wuthering Heights* was initially criticized for its violent, passionate nature, although it has since come to be regarded as one of the greatest novels in the English language. Both novels contain classic Gothic elements. In *Jane Eyre*, for example, the title character becomes a governess at an old mansion filled with secrets and strange occurrences, including a fire set by a mysterious figure. The Gothic elements of *Wuthering Heights*—including ghosts, wild weather, and remote landscapes—help to establish an eerie atmosphere in which is related the story of the terrible yet heroic Heathcliff, a man obsessed with the woman he loves.

Like the Brontës, American author Nathaniel Hawthorne wrote in the Gothic tradition. The descendant of a judge who took part in the Salem witch trials of 1692 (during which several people were imprisoned or hanged as punishment for being witches), Hawthorne featured witchcraft, curses, and the supernatural or seemingly supernatural in many of his works. The villain, Roger

< 32 >

Film versions of the Frankenstein story—from the early 1900s to today—have often been based on theatrical adaptations and spinoffs

Hawthorne was familiar with the history of witchcraft (and its associated persecution) in New England, having been born in Salem, Massachusetts.

Chillingworth, in Hawthorne's masterpiece *The Scarlet Letter* (1850), for example, possesses an apparently demonic ability to torture the young minister who has fathered a child with Chillingworth's wife. *The House of the Seven Gables* (1851) tells the story of a cursed family, while "Young Goodman Brown" (1835) features a witch's ceremony. In the latter, the horror evoked is largely psychological, as the protagonist is left wondering if the ceremony was real or only a dream. Hawthorne's psychological focus was an important precursor of later developments in horror, and his haunting descriptions influenced later horror masters such as H. P. Lovecraft.

Irish author Joseph Sheridan Le Fanu began writing ghost stories in 1838 while studying law—which he never practiced, choosing instead to become a writer. Le Fanu's novel *Uncle Silas* (1864) creates an air of impending doom as it relates the story of a young woman forced to live with her wicked uncle. Much of the story's dark atmosphere derives from Le Fanu's artful descriptions of the weather: "It was darkening rapidly; a mass of black clouds stood piled in the west, through the chasms of which was still reflected a pale metallic lustre. The drawing-room was already very dark; but some streaks of this cold light fell upon a black figure." Although *Uncle Silas* contains few supernatural elements, Le Fanu's shorter works are ranked among the best ghost stories of the period, and his vampire tale "Carmilla" (1872) was an important influence on Bram Stoker's *Dracula*.

By the turn of the 20th century, the Gothic influence could still be felt in horror literature, including in many of the short stories of Henry James. Although generally regarded as a realistic novelist, James also penned a number of psychologically complex ghost stories. Born in America, James later moved to Paris and then London, producing 20 novels and 112 short stories, along with a number of nonfiction volumes, in his 51-year literary career. Among his most famous short works is the 1898 novella (short novel) *The Turn of the Screw*, a ghost story that takes place in an eerie old country house. The governess of the house believes that the spirits of two dead servants are controlling the children who live there. Despite the apparently supernatural elements of the work, many critics believe that the narrator is actually insane—and thus the tale she relates is unreliable. The alternate readings of the work have made it one of the most hotly debated horror stories ever.

By contrast, the ghosts in English author M. R. James's stories are clearly meant to be real. A number of James's stories are set in Suffolk, the eastern English county where James grew up, or at King's College in Cambridge, England, where James served as provost (an administrator). A medieval scholar, James developed the antiquarian ghost story, a tale that focuses on objects from the past, such as books, that have evil hidden within them. These objects are collected by the stories' protagonists, who unwittingly release the horror. In "Count Magnus" (1904), a collector named Mr. Wraxall expresses a wish to see inside the copper coffin of an old noble known as Count Magnus. Suddenly, the padlock on the coffin falls off, startling Wraxall: "I stooped to pick it up, and ... before I had raised myself there was a sound of metal hinges creaking, and I distinctly saw the lid shifting upwards." Soon afterward, Wraxall is found dead. Yet James never describes exactly who Count Magnus is or how or why he has killed Wraxall.

< 36 >

A good ghost story often depends on its degree of believability,
or how convincingly it persuades the reader that a ghost could be real.

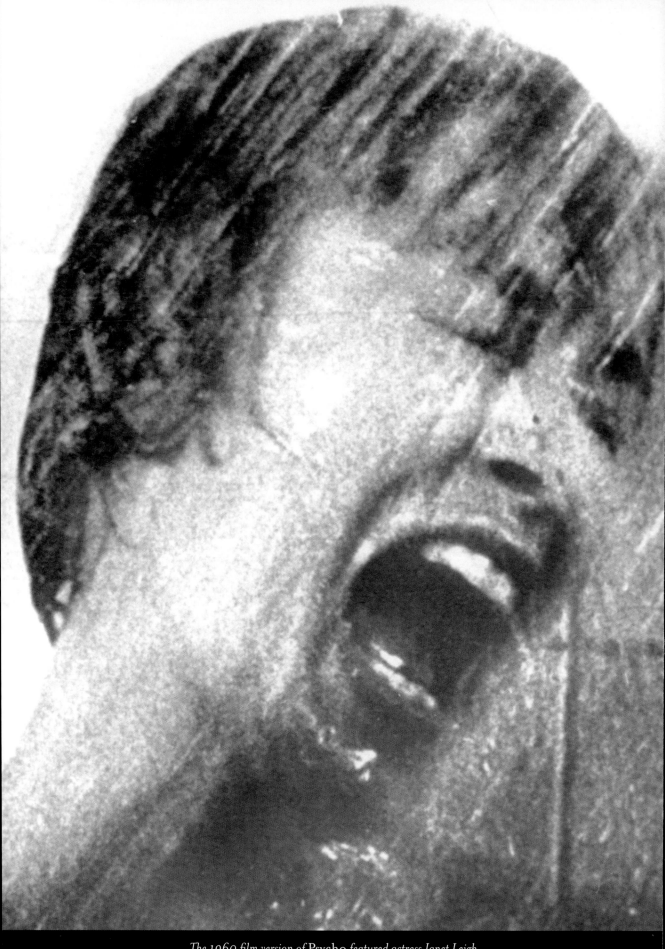

The 1960 film version of **Psycho** *featured actress Janet Leigh*

He does not wish to horrify readers with gruesome descriptions; instead, James believed that a good ghost story should make readers feel "pleasantly uncomfortable." Despite the appearance of antiquities in his works, James kept his settings contemporary. His style is neither high-strung nor melodramatic in the Gothic mode but rather leisurely and restrained, and his characters are typically cheerful or unemotional rather than hysterical or insane.

Among James's admirers was American author H. P. Lovecraft, who began reading horror fiction as a child and was enchanted by tales of history and Gothic terror. In his own works, Lovecraft combined the Gothic with an invented mythology to form the subgenre of cosmic horror. Although Lovecraft did not group his short stories together as a series, later writers categorized about 13 of them into a set that came to be known as the Cthulhu Mythos because of their common focus on a fictional universe in which an alien race of powerful beings (among whom was one named Cthulhu) once controlled Earth. Although Lovecraft's stories did not meet with success during his lifetime, he is today regarded as one of the most influential 20th-century horror writers. Both during and after Lovecraft's lifetime, his fictional world inspired several authors to create new tales within the mythos.

One of those writers was American Robert Bloch, whom Lovecraft mentored. After writing a number of short stories in the Cthulhu Mythos cycle, Bloch turned from Lovecraft's cosmic horror to his own style, becoming most famous for *Psycho* (1959), a novel with a human "monster" rather than a supernatural one. After killing his mother and her lover, the character of Norman Bates develops a split personality, half of which takes on the persona of his mother. The "mother" part of his personality dominates Bates and goes so far as to kill a young woman staying at the motel he manages. Bloch provides

A HORROR CLASSIC

Published in 1897, Bram Stoker's Dracula *has become one of the most enduring and influential of all horror novels. Told through a series of letters and journal entries written by the story's protagonists, the tale centers on the evil vampire Count Dracula. The vampire takes the English lawyer Jonathan Harker prisoner in his Transylvanian castle and later travels to England, where he feeds on the blood of Harker's wife, Mina. The vampire also forces Mina to drink of his own blood in order to create a bond that he uses to control her. Eventually, a group led by the vampire-hunter Abraham Van Helsing tracks and destroys Dracula, saving Mina.*

Stoker's story contains a number of innovations striking for that time. The tale takes place in a contemporary, rather than historical, setting. In addition, it provides no explanation of Dracula's origin or reasons for choosing his victims. Both of these devices would be adopted by future horror writers. Perhaps most influential of all, though, was Stoker's description of Dracula. Although the count at first appears to be a charming man, Jonathan Harker later finds him lying in a coffin-like box, "looking as if his youth had been half renewed, for the white hair and moustache were changed to dark iron-grey; the cheeks were fuller, and the white skin seemed ruby-red underneath; the mouth was redder than ever, for on the lips were gouts of fresh blood, which trickled from the corners of the mouth and ran over the chin and neck." Such a depiction of a vampire's physical characteristics would set the standard for many future bloodthirsty creatures.

< 40 >

The traditional image
of Count Dracula is
as a pale-faced,
human-like character
featuring sharp fangs and
a flowing, black cloak.

an intense description of the scene (made even more popular in the Alfred Hitchcock-directed movie that came out in 1960): "The roar [of the shower] was deafening, and the room was beginning to steam up.... At first, when the shower curtains parted, the steam obscured the face.... It was the face of a crazy old woman. Mary started to scream, and then the curtains parted further and a hand appeared, holding a butcher's knife. It was the knife that, a moment later, cut off her scream. And her head." Bloch's style—which relied on suspense and surprise—influenced later writers such as Stephen King.

While the reader stands apart from the character of Norman Bates, watching him with growing horror, readers of Anne Rice's fiction are taken into the world of her monsters, who often narrate their own stories. Although Rice began penning stories as a child, she did not publish her first novel until 1976, after the death of her five-year-old daughter. In her grief, Rice poured *Interview with the Vampire* onto the page, creating in it a young girl who gains immortality as a vampire. The book became the first in the 10-novel series known as the Vampire Chronicles. Rice also published a number of other horror works, including *The Mummy, or Ramses the Damned* (1989) and *The Witching Hour* (1990).

Among the most prolific and best-known of horror writers today is Stephen King, who has written nearly 50 novels, as well as a number of short stories, novellas, and nonfiction works. King's stories have featured nearly every monster imaginable, including vampires, ghosts, rabid dogs, demons, and even a young woman with telekinetic powers (in his first novel, *Carrie*, published in 1974). Inspired by the American Gothic tradition, King wrote a number of works in the Gothic style, including *'Salem's Lot* (1975) and *The Shining* (1977). In spite of their often supernatural elements, King's works usually take place in seemingly normal suburban towns, often in Maine, where the author lives. In many cases,

< 42 >

the horror builds slowly, as King crafts a sense of foreboding and fear. In *Misery* (1987), for example, terror mounts as the mentally unstable serial killer Annie Wilkes proceeds from imprisoning injured author Paul Sheldon to chopping off his foot with an ax.

King, who continues to write today, has been joined by a number of new voices in horror fiction. Among them is Clive Barker, an English writer whose works often focus on physical horror and gruesome acts of violence, as in *Mister B. Gone* (2007), the diary of a demon who has left hell. Other authors, such as American Mary SanGiovanni, have shifted the focus back to psychological horror in novels such as *The Hollower* (2007), in which the monster plays on its victims' greatest weaknesses, seeking out those with severe doubts and insecurities and causing some to commit suicide.

From the supernatural occurrences of the Gothic novel to the inner dread of the psychological horror story, the genre has undergone a number of changes and developments in its nearly 250-year history. Old characters such as vampires have been reused and reinvented, while new horrors—such as computers gone bad—have begun to appear on the page. But while monsters, settings, and techniques may vary from one work to another, horror stories through the ages have had the same goal—to give you, the reader, a good fright.

< 45 >

abbey: a Christian convent (home for nuns) or monastery (home for monks)

archaeologist: a person who studies ancient societies by examining what they left behind, such as buildings, records, and tools

archetypes: typical examples or models

cloisters: covered walkways built along the outside of a building around a central courtyard

contemporary: living or existing at the same time as someone or something else

ecological: having to do with the environment and the interactions of living organisms with their surroundings

genre: a category in which a literary work can be classified on the basis of style, technique, or subject matter

governess: a woman who is a private teacher and caretaker who teaches children in their own homes

parodying: copying or imitating in a humorous way

point of view: the perspective from or attitude with which the narrator of a literary work sees events

protagonists: the main characters in a work of fiction

psychological: having to do with the mind and effects on the mind

relics: parts of a deceased person's body or objects that belonged to the person that are kept as objects of honor or worship

sociopaths: people having a severe personality disorder characterized by behavior that is dangerous to others and lacking a feeling of remorse

Spanish Inquisition: a court made up of Catholic officials in Spain that, from about 1478 to 1834, sought to identify and punish those who held beliefs contrary to the Church's teaching

supernatural: relating to objects or powers that have no natural explanation and seem to exist outside natural laws

symbolism: the use of one thing, such as a character or color, to represent something else, often an idea, such as love or evil

sympathetic: arousing sympathy or approval

telekinetic: having the ability to move objects using only the mind

ventriloquist: a person with the ability to make his or her voice sound as if it comes from somewhere other than him- or herself

Western: coming from or having to do with the part of the world that includes Europe and North and South America, where culture has been influenced by ancient Greek and Roman civilizations as well as Christianity

WEBSITES

Dracula's Homepage: Traits of the Vampire
http://www.ucs.mun.ca/~emiller/traits.html
Discover many of the most telling characteristics of a vampire, specifically of Count Dracula.

Edgar Allan Poe Museum: Students
http://www.poemuseum.org/students.php
Find out more about Edgar Allan Poe's life, and watch a video of "The Tell-Tale Heart."

Frankenstein: Penetrating the Secrets of Nature
http://www.nlm.nih.gov/exhibition/frankenstein/preface.html
Learn more about the topics and themes contained in Mary Shelley's Frankenstein.

Stephen King: The Office
http://www.stephenking.com/the_office.html
Get to know author Stephen King through this interactive virtual tour of his office.

Every effort has been made to ensure that these sites are suitable for children, that they have educational value, and that they contain no inappropriate material. However, because of the nature of the Internet, it is impossible to guarantee that these sites will remain active indefinitely or that their contents will not be altered.

SELECTED BIBLIOGRAPHY

Barron, Neil, ed. *Horror Literature: A Reader's Guide.* New York: Garland Publishing, 1990.

Fonseca, Anthony, and June Michele Pulliam. *Hooked on Horror: A Guide to Reading Interests in Horror Fiction.* Englewood, Colo.: Libraries Unlimited, 1999.

———. *Hooked on Horror III: A Guide to Reading Interests.* Westport, Conn.: Libraries Unlimited, 2009.

King, Stephen. *Danse Macabre.* New York: Everest House, 1981.

MacNee, Marie, ed. *Science Fiction, Fantasy, and Horror Writers.* 2 vols. New York: UXL, 1995.

Saricks, Joyce G. *The Readers' Advisory Guide to Genre Fiction.* Chicago: American Library Association, 2001.

Stuprich, Michael, ed. *Horror.* San Diego: Greenhaven Press, 2001.

Tymn, Marshall B. *Horror Literature: A Core Collection and Reference Guide.* New York: R. R. Bowker Company, 1981.

< 47 >